SELECTED POEMS
1942-1968

By the same author

Speak with the Sun
The Miracle of Mullion Hill
Poems
Evening under Lamplight (short stories)

SELECTED POEMS
1942-1968

David Campbell

Angus and Robertson

ACKNOWLEDGMENTS

For permission to reprint poems in this selection
not previously published in book form
acknowledgements are due to the *Australian,
Australian Letters, Meanjin, Overland,
Poetry Australia, Southerly,
Sydney Morning Herald, Texas Quarterly.*
Poems reprinted from *Speak with the Sun*
are published by arrangement with
Chatto and Windus Ltd; those from *Poems*
by arrangement with Edwards & Shaw Pty Ltd.

First published in 1968 by
ANGUS & ROBERTSON LTD
221 George Street, Sydney
54 Bartholomew Close, London
107 Elizabeth Street, Melbourne

Published with the assistance of the Commonwealth Literary Fund

Registered in Australia for transmission by post as a book
Printed in Australia by Edwards & Shaw Pty Ltd, Sydney

Preface

Making a selection of poetry is like losing weight, a cutting down to size. But though there may be some enterprise in going naked, little can be said for appearing as a skeleton in public. Time and fashion will have their say soon enough.

All the poems here were written during the past twenty-five years. There are a few I like that I have left out and there are a great many more that I hope to write. I have crossed some *t*'s, made minor alterations where I seemed to have missed the point, and done some shuffling for the sake of clarity. Otherwise the poems are as they were and in the same order as when they first went out to the hawks and doves.

A poet does not always write the sort of poetry he would like to write ("the full proud sail") so that his theory may differ from his practice. His poems that are any good are partly given. What he does with these "gifts" is, of course, up to him: he may increase their stature with a little thought and the use of a compass; he may even change as his world changes, and his poetry, if it keeps up, will change too. But if he gazes too aquilinely in one direction or follows every ankle, he should take care that his Muse is not pulling faces behind his back. When in doubt, a poet should write nursery rhymes.

The section *Talking to Strangers* has not been published in a book before. Most of the thefts in it from other languages cannot be called even imitations with much honesty: I have used what I needed to make my own poems. So from a fifteenth century courtly chanson I have got two rough bush songs, and made sonnets from free verse and prose poems. But when you try this sort of thing with poets like Hérédia, you accept obvious risks.

DAVID CAMPBELL

Contents

Lyrical

Harry Pearce

I sat beside the red stock route
And chewed a blade of bitter grass
And saw in mirage on the plain
A bullock wagon pass.
Old Harry Pearce was with his team.
"The flies are bad," I said to him.

The leaders felt his whip. It did
Me good to hear old Harry swear,
And in the heat of noon it seemed
His bullocks walked on air.
Suspended in the amber sky
They hauled the wool to Gundagai.

He walked in Time across the plain,
An old man walking in the air;
For years he wandered in my brain,
And now he lodges here.
And he may drive his cattle still
When Time with us has had his will.

The Stockman

The sun was in the summer grass,
The coolabahs were twisted steel:
The stockman paused beneath their shade
And sat upon his heel,
And with the reins looped through his arm
He rolled tobacco in his palm.

His horse stood still. His cattle dog
Tongued in the shadow of the tree,
And for a moment on the plain
Time waited for the three.
And then the stockman licked his fag
And Time took up his solar swag.

I saw the stockman mount and ride
Across the mirage on the plain;
And still that timeless moment brought
Fresh ripples to my brain:
It seemed in that distorting air
I saw his grandson sitting there.

Winter Stock Route

Here where red dust rose
To raddle sheep and men
And the kelpie tongued at noon,
Silence has come again.
The great-boled gumtrees bow
Beneath their load of snow.

The drover and his dray
Have gone; and on this hill
I find myself alone
And Time standing still.
Printless the white road lies
Before my quiet skis.

But where my skis trace
Their transient snow furrow,
For generations both
Man and beast will follow.
Now in this winter passage
I cross the deserted stage.

Spring Hares

There is a stranger on the stock route.
See his red beard and eyes of flame!
The sky's his swag; the magpies shout
Across the continent his name:
It is the sun! It is the dawn!—
Bless the day that I was born.

There are two boxers through the gum-trees;
Their shadows spar on the far hill,
Counter and close. What giants are these?
Surprised, a pair of hares stand still.
It's a fine thing at your front gate
To see such angry lovers mate.

Bill is out on the red stallion;
His piebald mob crops blades of fire.
Trees burn, leaves melt; in conflagration
The big buck hare has his desire
Where the red ridge meets the spring sky,
Locked in the sun's irradiant eye.

The Trapper's Song

"In the bracken country,"
The trapper said to me,
"I am abroad before the sun;
The only man to see
The first light liquefy the leaves
On every standing tree.

"From the early sunlight
The magpie takes her note.
Her voice is heard, then like the bird
I loosen up my throat;
And she and I sing to the day
A song we have by rote.

"It is an idle lyric"—
The trapper cocked an eye;
"One singing from a bracken brake,
The other from the sky,
That bird and beast are at their spring
And may give death the lie.

"I gather up my rabbits
And down the bracken lane
I sing a song that life is young
And scorn the mortal strain
Of rabbits nodding at my belt
That say my song is vain."

Old Tom Dances

The grass is bleached like a barmaid's hair,
As soft as her arms in the evening air,
And old Tom dances in the failing light,
A foot in day and a foot in night.

Old Tom dances; he skips like a hare;
And the rising moon had better beware
For Tom and his pockets are stuffed with rum
And he dares the moon and 'em all to come.

"Whoa there, bullocks!" he tells his feet;
"There's rum in the billy, there's rum for meat.
Up there, Baldy! Up there, Roan!"
And he talks to his feet in a bullocky's tone.

Who is that peeping through sunset eyes
As the sun sinks and the stars rise?
He thought that boy forty years dead
For he pulled the blankets over his head.

The boy looks out, his kelpie fears
Forgotten, forgotten the twisted years
And the fiend who stares from the dam's still glass;
And he lies in locks of moonlit grass.

The Kidney and the Wren

A MELODRAMA

The jackass laughs in the white light;
The silence of the noon
Is shattered. From a crooked tree
He cackles like a loon.
The crow throws on his villainous cloak
In the footlights of the sun.

And though the lark, the thrush, the wren,
May hiss from stalls of briar,
The black crow looks from lidded eyes,
His voice is colder than the skies,
He pecks a young lamb's kidney out
And throws it to the choir.

And lo! The smallest little wren
Quits hissing, quits the thicket;
Sun glints from avaricious eye;
Her beak is quick to pick it.
A golden hawk drops from the sun;
The wren and lamb are one.

The jackass laughed in the white light;
The silence of the noon was shattered.
I asked him what the moral was?
He said, "As if it mattered!"
He laughed aloud: "It was kid-stakes;
My favourite heroines are snakes."

Small-town Gladys

There are rows of bottles against the glass;
I look between and my hair's blonde grass,
My lips are berries and my skin is cream
And I fill my frock to the very brim
And twirl a curl when the sportsmen pass —
And I'm a good girl, I am.

They call me Glad and say I'm a queen.
I look in the glass and my eyes are green
And they talk to men though they make no sound
For it's love that makes the world go round;
But go too far and I say, "Go on;
I am a good girl, I am."

In every novel I'm Lady Jane,
I use the book as a wicked fan,
And I sit on a stool and my fingers knit
A web to snare a sportsman's wit;
And they look at me as they look for rain,
But I'm a good girl, I am.

Under the willows, under the night,
Where schoolboys spy and the parson might,
I am the moon that rules the tides
Of men. And I shake and hold my sides
And I say, "My make-up's an awful sight —
And I'm a good girl, I am."

"Race Book, Race Book,
Race Book for Randwick!"

Place your bet in the paddock with the flushed bookmaker,
That marsupial man who cups fat fists to call
The odds and lays the field for any taker;
Come, down your beer; come to the favourite's stall.

The chestnut stallion stands there like a king,
Pride in his carriage, eagles in his eye,
His mane the wind. Sun smooths his colouring
With gentle hand, falls flat on passers-by.

The groom stands in the shade. Twin horses ride
The pupils of his eyes. This stable boy
Scorns the lean tipster with a borrowed pride,
His whisper, "Is the red the real McCoy?"

He is holding his joy in hand with a tight rein
Until the field turns into the straight for home
And the crowd stands up. He fondles his horse in pain
As once he fondled him on the tracks of Rome.

At the Sheep-dog Trials

What ancestors unite
Here in this red and white
Kelpie to define
His symmetry of line,

As crouched in burning dust
He halts both Time and beast?
The wethers stamp the ground,
At his will turn around.

He is of collie stock:
Austerity of rock
Lent his mind and bone
The toughness of its stone;

And though for Border flocks
The collie and the fox
Fought tooth to tooth, they joined
And have the kelpie coined

Whose ears acutely set
Across the centuries yet
Hear the concordant sound
Of coupled horn and hound;

And as the moon the tides
The hidden vixen guides
With craft the blood that strains
And surges in his veins.

Those who stand and stare
At cripples in the fair
Have not the eyes to see
His blood's dignity

Where old adversaries meet,
As now on velvet feet
He moves to his master's call,
In action classical.

Let Each Ripen

Where the horse and horseman go
Iron is clamorous on stone,
Spark and heavenly bluebell grow.
World enough for flesh and bone.
The black mare in the blue pool
Stamps her image and is still.

Where the tree would spread her bough
Cloud masses fill the chart;
There the skilled explorer now
Satisfies and steels the heart.
The aircraft sings in the thinning air,
Climbs the still, momentous stair.

Let the living horseman ride:
Sweet and sensuous is earth's breath;
Scorned by the pilot in his pride,
It will open at his death.
Before his final bed is made
Let each ripen in his trade.

The Possum and the Moon

I

Where a twisted tree
Split the rough sandstone,
I stood at night and heard
A possum scold the moon.

I listened for the cock
Who would call my dead
Grandfather from his grave
To my grandmother's bed.

I waited for the magpie
An hour before the dawn
To sing "Tan tara, boys!"
On old John Bax's horn.

I lifted up my hand
And made my ear a cup:
The skewbald dingo slept
At Brigalow Gap.

The only sounds I heard
That hour before the light
Were the tide in the leaves,
The possum's cry to the night.

II

I heard the possum cry
Beneath the yellow moon.
I said, "That moon was made
From this same sandstone."

The moon looked through the trees
And where her shadows stood,
Blackmen sprang upright;
They filled the ancient wood.

A tide ran through the leaves;
Otherwise a still
Hush lay on the bush
Where the shadows fell.

Like a lubra the land
Lay quiet, indifferent.
The shadows stole to the trees
At the moon's ascent.

Conroy's Gap

The lorry climbs towards Conroy's Gap;
The driver and the moon are full,
For while he drank at The Shadow of Death
The moon lay down on his load of wool
And with a bale-hook in her hair
Like a willing girl she is sleeping there.

— He heard the trooper at the door,
He heard the barmaid catch her breath
And when the Swagman leapt the rails
He heard the rider laugh at death
Who rode as mountain horsemen ride
With Darby Munro at his side.—

The lorry moves past walls of stone;
The driver yawns and rubs his eyes:
A convict in a tailored suit
Is picking shale on the iron rise
And singing in the bitter cold,
"I dig for truth in chains of gold."

The possum's eyes return the glare
Of headlights; dingoes hunt the hills
And pick the moonlight from dry bones
That once stood up in Burke and Wills.
As bristles stand on the dingo's hide —
The bones knit up; Burke thumbs a ride.

"Both beer and girls I loved," he said,
"And yet my mind would not be still
Despite the inadequacy of flesh
To execute the spirit's will
In city or on desolate plain.
Wills, up man! Time to strive again."

The lightning strides across the ridge;
Wills strides between the falling steel;
A tommy-gun is in his hand
And men in green are at his heel,

While those beneath the Flemish grass
Cry, "You'll be sorry," as they pass.

The lorry crosses Conroy's Gap.
Feel for the butt behind your ear;
Here are the matches, strike and cup
Your lean face in the red flare
And blink the mirage from your brain
Where Harry walks on moonshine.

Soldier's Song

Though I march until I drop
And my bed is sand,
I have filled the desert's cup,
Harvested its land;
And this I learned from the desert wind,
From the sphinx it blows:
The Murray's source is in the mind
And at a word it flows.

Though I climb the bitter rock,
Jungle for a bed,
I can muster such a flock
As never Falkiner bred;
And this I learned from the tropic wind
Where the giant storm grows:
The Murray's source is in the mind
And at a word it flows.

Men in Green

There were fifteen men in green,
Each with a tommy-gun,
Who leapt into my plane at dawn;
We rose to meet the sun.

We set our course towards the east
And climbed into the day
Till the ribbed jungle underneath
Like a giant fossil lay.

We climbed towards the distant range
Where two white paws of cloud
Clutched at the shoulders of the pass;
The green men laughed aloud.

They did not fear the ape-like cloud
That climbed the mountain crest
And hung from twisted ropes of air
With thunder in its breast.

They did not fear the summer's sun
In whose hot centre lie
A hundred hissing cannon shells
For the unwatchful eye.

And when on Dobadura's field
We landed, each man raised
His thumb towards the open sky;
But to their right I gazed.

For fifteen men in jungle green
Rose from the kunai grass
And came towards the plane. My men
In silence watched them pass;
It seemed they looked upon themselves
In Time's prophetic glass.

Oh, there were some leaned on a stick
And some on stretchers lay,
But few walked on their own two feet
In the early green of day.

They had not feared the ape-like cloud
That climbed the mountain crest;
They had not feared the summer's sun
With bullets for their breast.

Their eyes were bright, their looks were dull,
Their skin had turned to clay.
Nature had met them in the night
And stalked them in the day.

And I think still of men in green
On the Soputa track
With fifteen spitting tommy-guns
To keep a jungle back.

Greek Boy and Girl with Rifles
1947

Against the vivid drop of sky
See where this sullen couple stand,
The tiger lashed within his eye,
The orchard crushed within her hand.

Here on this dusty road in Greece
The snipers' summer-lightning gleams
And each man greets his brother's face
Each time he slides the bolt and aims
Or wounds the one for whom he burns,
The darling of his mind and lust;
And voices plead within the loins
And cry a warning from the dust.

Oh you who stand above the plain
And wear a clouded human face
Are counters in a dead man's brain
Or guardians of a foreign peace;
But stand as you have ever stood,
Aggressor and victim of all wars;
And evening glistens with your blood
And streams are turbulent with your tears.

The Tally

What is it your fingers tell
When you stop to cross the street?
— What I have I would not have
As he knows who loves me well;
The only kisses that I crave
Glorify my will's defeat,
Said Joan and walked on.

What is it your fingers tell
When the grey rain is falling down?
— Light the light and press the bell,
Step into a velvet gown;
Sitting here before the glass
I defy the years that pass,
Said Jean in spring green.

What is it your fingers tell
When the factory whistles sound?
— I have got a dress as well,
Sewn, hemmed, and made to fit;
I will wear it with an air
Till I have a foot of ground
And no use for it.

The Forking Tree

I said to my love, "Come with me
Where like lightning stands the tree."
But my love drew back in fright:
"There is a savage under it;
See his naked back and thigh,
See the mica of his eye
And the gesture of his arm —
And my father's house is warm."

I took her hand. "Come," I said,
"Though the leaves glow white and red."
But a convict sat in chains
Suffering the world's pains
Underneath the forking tree,
Hate and wonder in his eye:
"Look," he said, "beyond the rise
Wrapt in glory, China lies."

I said to my love, "Come," again.
The sun struck on the bitter plain
Where the lonely swagman stood,
And his murmur chilled the blood:
I have walked the twisted track,
Rods of sunlight on my back,
And I walked so far alone
That my brain returned to stone.

I took her pretty hand. She came
Where the fire cured her shame
And the naked man was hushed
For he brought us all we wished
Peddling a hundred wares
From the misty hemispheres;
And our minds shook off the spell
Of the swagman's lonely tale.

Speak with the Sun

From a wreck of tree in the wash of night
Glory, glory, sings the bird;
Across ten thousand years of light
His creative voice is heard.

Wide on a tide of wind are set
Warp and woof of silvered air;
But the song slips through the net
To where the myriad galaxies are.

And to the heartbeats of the light,
Now from the deepness of the glade
Well up the bubbles of delight:
Of such stuff the stars were made.

FROM *The Miracle of Mullion Hill*

I

The End of Exploring

See! down the red road by the brown tree
The gate leans wide like morning. Here's winter's green;
Here are summer's bleached affairs; and here between
Rain work and wind work, the road winds free.

The shed is slabbed with shimmer. Fence-posts go
Hill-high for shadows. Ben's on his bright chain:
And it's the dog's limit, the green cock's strain;
And the road lies hard and open towards the snow.

But why go? The time waits deep for summer
With the grain, for the ringed shade and sheep
Cropping the silence while the swagmen sleep,
Though on the height the ice-etched symbols glimmer.

And the road? Go then; and smothered in the snow,
Or on the violet ridge where the ice-trees burn,
Trust to your lucky heart you may return
With love to dog-bark, gate, and sweet cock-crow.

Windy Gap

As I was going through Windy Gap
A hawk and a cloud hung over the map.

The land lay bare and the wind blew loud
And the hawk cried out from the heart of the cloud,

"Before I fold my wings in sleep
I'll pick the bones of your travelling sheep,

"For the leaves blow back and the wintry sun
Shows the tree's white skeleton."

A magpie sat in the tree's high top
Singing a song on Windy Gap

That streamed far down to the plain below
Like a shaft of light from a high window.

From the bending tree he sang aloud,
And the sun shone out of the heart of the cloud

And it seemed to me as we travelled through
That my sheep were the notes that trumpet blew.

And so I sing this song of praise
For travelling sheep and blowing days.

Snow-gums

Moonlight and snow and snow-gums:
After much living turn, return
To the soul's climate, to cold forms
Wind cuts in ice and stone.

There stand like Socrates
Barefoot through the winter's night;
Burn in snowbound silences
As the trees hold the moonlight.

The powdered bloom along the bough
Wavers like a candle's breath;
Where snow falls softly into snow
Iris and rivers have their birth.

Ariel

Frost and snow, frost and snow:
The old ram scratches with a frozen toe
At silver tussocks in the payable mist
And stuffs his belly like a treasure chest.

His tracks run green up the mountainside
Where he throws a shadow like a storm-cloud's hide;
He has tossed the sun in a fire of thorns,
And a little bird whistles between his horns.

"Sweet-pretty-creature!" sings the matchstick bird,
And on height and in chasm his voice is heard;
Like a bell of ice or the crack of the frost
It rings in the ears of his grazing host.

"Sweet-pretty-creature!" While all is as still
As the bird on the ram on the frozen hill,
O the wagtail warms to his tiny art
And glaciers move through the great beast's heart.

Dance of Flame and Shadow

CALIBAN CHORUS

All who walk in the sun's light
Throw a shadow. Of a shade,
Hooded angel of the hush,
Are these leaping terrors made
That dance upon the walls of flesh.

You have done and left undone.
Let the briar but pluck the sleeve,
And naked on the precipice
See the modest take their leave.
Snap a thread and come to this.

Snap a thread and come to this:
If the images that bless
Fade like mirage on the air,
Stepping through the looking-glass
Pause and leave a shadow there.

Who set the hearth within the heart,
Candles winking in the mind
To book and bedtime children? Ask
The ape behind the window-blind,
The murderer in the comic mask.

Here and there we shadows greet,
Doze and shuffle, hang like poor
Relations on a strap of breath
And bolt our pie-crust at the door
Who fear the rag-and-bone-man, truth.

The Beggars

Lear and blind Œdipus
Play with birds and butterflies.
Naked we come and go
Under the terrible skies.
Lord, have mercy upon us.

He has luck who can
Follow temperate streams of blood
Through a chequered fallow land
And where his father stood,
Leave his shadow on the plan.

Blessed if beneath
The grey towers of the mind
Dreaming where the coloured light
Weaves its web, he find
Satisfaction for his death.

Yet with wind and rain
Butterflies and beggars ride;
A lightning cleaves the heart,
And there is so much pride
They must seek their death again.

Who Points the Swallow

Love who points the swallow home
And scarves the russet at his throat,
Dreaming in the needle's eye,
Guide us through the maze of glass
Where the forceful cannot pass,
With your silent clarity.

There where blood and sap are one,
Thrush's heart and daisy's root
Keep the measure of the dance,
Though within their cage of bone
Griefs and tigers stalk alone,
Locked in private arrogance.

Lay the shadow of our fear
With the brilliance of your light,
Naked we can meet the storm,
Travellers who journeyed far
To find you at our own front door,
O love who points the swallow home.

In Summer's Tree

In summer's yellow tree
The bird sings low;
There my thoughts are leaves,
But he sings from the shadow.

Under thought he sings
And he locks the hot summer
Like a spring's reflections
In his words of amber.

One world is of time,
And the other of vision,
And the magpie's song
Brings peace and fusion:

For now the sharp leaves
On the tree are still,
And the great blond paddocks
Come down from the hill.

Night Sowing

O gentle, gentle land
Where the green ear shall grow,
Now you are edged with light:
The moon has crisped the fallow,
The furrows run with night.

This is the season's hour:
While couples are in bed,
I sow the paddocks late,
Scatter like sparks the seed
And see the dark ignite.

O gentle land, I sow
The heart's living grain.
Stars draw their harrows over,
Dews send their melting rain:
I meet you as a lover.

The High Plains

EVERLASTING FLOWERS

On the high plains by Dairyman,
If you look up, you'll see
Peter Quinn and his hollow mare
Caught in a spider-tree:

Along the banks of Dairyman
The paper-daisies grow
That lock the sunlight in their palm
As they go under snow.

There summertime and Dairyman
Talk to themselves in sleep;
The winds blow round the mountainside
And Quinn goes round the sheep,

Who, from the pools of Dairyman,
Has learned the dreamer's power
To shut up mountains in his mind
As the seed holds the flower.

And though snow covers Dairyman,
Listen and you may hear
The water talking to the stones
Like Peter to his mare.

The Monaro

Willy Gray will sit and stare
On One Tree Hill the whole day long
And green grass-parrots fly in at his ear
And lay their eggs of rounded song
Leaving them there for the words to hatch
Like floating seed from the thistle patch.

Willy Gray has a ten-mile stare
And his eyes are droving with a dream of sheep
Down raddled stock-routes to tread white air
Where Willy Gray has a thought as deep
And rounded as a river-stone —
And over the paddocks goes the daylight moon.

Willy Gray has a lover's eye
And it goes over the twin bare hills
And the blond paddocks to the bleached sky
Until it has come to a thought that fills
His mind with tenderness for this wild
Upland country and her suckling child.

Words and Lovers

The terror of God, of thought without
The sweet coupling of words and lovers!
A disembodied spirit dreams
In windy frames and vacant forms
Who sightless seeks a face for grief
And flesh to rid himself of love.

In the sea, on the shore, dreaming within
The cave of seeds, his children curl
And hear shell-voices whisper long
Forgotten words that sleepers sing
Where all the past is and the past
Wakes at their waking or is lost.

Take water, mineral. Take heed,
Nothing is made of nothing. See
Thought's green articulation, dreams
Putting on flesh — so summer storms
Suck up the ocean. Even fears
Must beg of sense and music ears.

This is thought's miracle that word
Lies down with word and lover with lover.
The whirlwind courtship of great trees
Lovesick with honey, similes
That take in marriage, and lips that kiss,
Bear witness to thought's loneliness.

Ephemerons

Out of the river's glass they come
To dance beneath the sally-tree,
Nymphs who call a moment home
Knowing the mirror's ecstasy
Where the blue crane and toppling hill
Stand for ever in the pool.

II

Song for the Cattle

Down the red stock route
Hock-deep in mirage
Rode the three black drovers
Singing to the cattle.

And with them a young woman,
Perhaps some squatter's daughter
From homestead or township,
Who turned her horse easily.

To my mind she was as beautiful
As the barmaid in Brewarrina
Who works at the Royal. Men
Ride all day to see her.

Fine-boned as a brigalow
Yet ample as a granary,
She has teeth good for laughing
Or biting an apple.

I'm thinking of quitting
My mountain selection,
The milking at morning
And the lonely axe-echoes;

Of swapping my slab hut
For a rolled-up blanket
And heading north-westward
For a life in the saddle —

For the big mobs trailing
Down the empty stock routes,
A horned moon at evening
And songs round the campfire.

Yes, I'll soon be drinking
At the Royal in Brewarrina
And ambling through mirage
With the squatter's daughter.

Donoghoe and the Wattle

Old Jack Donoghoe
Fossicking for colour
Down by the Bullock Head
Found a tree of yellow.

"Wish," said the wattle-tree;
"What will you buy?"
"Three blonde waitresses
And a quart of whisky."

"Wish, Jack Donoghoe."
"I shall live
In a yellow town-house
Beside the Tiv.;

"And there will be music
And johnny-cakes and janes
And a coloured rouseabout
To hand round the wines."

"Wish, Jack Donoghoe."
"And when I am dead,
A bird in a wattle-tree
Singing overhead,

"That I may find
When my veins are cold
Where the niggard wattle-tree
Gets her gold."

Kelly and the Crow

I

Where's John Kelly?
Kelly is lost
In whipstick scrub
And starlight frost.

A crow flew over;
"Kelly," he said,
"Flesh and blood
Will soon be dead —

"Follow me, Kelly."
And away he flew
Where the mirage water
Met the dew.

The Old Man Plain
Had one wall-eye,
And Kelly followed
The crow's cry

Of, "Kelly, Kelly,
You'll soon be dead,"
Until he came
To his old bark shed.

II

Kelly was dipping
The station ewes.
From a ringbarked tree
He heard the crow's

Cry of, "Kelly!
I want some meat.
Drown a sheep, Kelly,
For I must eat.

"Kelly, Kelly,
Drown a sheep
With your wooden crutch
In the narrow dip

"Or I'll pick your bones
When next you're lost."
And he stropped his beak
On a corner post.

But Kelly cried,
"Be damned if I do!
I'll drown no sheep
For a jumped-up crow;

"And I'll take good care
I'm not lost again
In whipstick scrub
On the Old Man Plain."

Jack Spring

The day the back lavatory
Went down the creek,
Boys looked from the orchard
And up strode Jack.

"There's ten bob in silver
For the first son of mine
To own that he pushed it
And speak like a man."

"Father, I did it.
I only meant
To ease her a little
And in she went.

"That's ten bob, father."
"Now hear me, son:
I've five white florins
For Washington

"And the father of a hiding
Unless you prove to me
The father of George Washington
Was in the cherry-tree."

Under the Coolabahs

Under the coolabahs
In their grey singlets
Shearers are dancing with
Barmaids in ringlets.

Firelight and kettle-drum,
Fiddler and trombone:
Here are pretty girls to dance
With anyone who's handsome.

Jenny dances to the moon
With a tray of schooners.
Put one down for Jenny, boys,
And her winter bloomers.

But the ringer takes his shears
And a holt of Jenny.
Sheep-oh! Wool away!
And she hasn't any.

Jenny cautions, "Have a care!"
Hunting for her mirror.
"I don't love you any more.
There, you gay deceiver!"

Then hey! for the rouseabout
And hey! for the ringer;
And hey! for the man to shout
For the next singer.

Come Live with Me

HE   Come live with me and we'll be drovers;
When stars are lambing in the rivers,
By couples we will count the sheep
Yet kiss before we go to sleep.

All summer down the Lachlan-side
We'll sing like Clancy as we ride
Till hawks hang charmed above the plain
And shearing-time comes in again.

For love of you I'll ring the shed,
And we'll have breakfast served in bed
By slattern maids in cotton caps,
And go to work at noon perhaps.

SHE   And in a basket I will keep
The skirtings of the finest sheep
For spinning tights for ballet-girls
With combs and cutters in their curls;

And they will dance at each smoke-oh
For your delight upon the toe
And bring you beer and violets
In garlands for your gallon hats.

With mistletoe I'll crown my hair
And sing most sweetly to the air,
"Since Time's a shearer, where's the sin
In kissing in the super-bin?"

Waiter and Cuckoo

Now each bush becomes a barmaid,
Mild and bitter blows the wind,
Lions stalk in cat and kitten,
And the waiter's girl is laid
Like a picnic in the shade.

Lambs walk in their mother's shadow,
Dance like napkins on the hill,
Stand upon the waiter's coat-tail
While his lady whispers, No!
I will love you if you do.

What's the pallid cuckoo cooking?
Laying stars in summer's well.
Come, my poppet, no one's looking
And the cuckoo will not tell
Whose note is silence in a shell.

Dawn Song

Now Dawn gets up as blond as birds,
The lucky man she marries
Will save a fortune on her dress
For wives discard with nakedness
A pretty pile of worries.

Just slap her in a spider-web
And never pay the spider;
Though he sits soaping like a Jew,
He'll get no more than's overdue
On guernseys for Godiva.

At foot she's ninety Leicester lambs,
Her soloists are thrushes
Who simply for a song arrange
Quotations from the stock-exchange
And sing them in the bushes.

But should these rural sophistries
Set men of business yawning,
She'll kiss her fingers once and say,
Good morning. Till another day —
But not before the morning.

Summer Comes with Colour

Summer comes with colour,
The wheat turns yellow
And in globes of light
Hares lope through the stubble

Where in shimmer to the knees
The trees cut their losses
And forgetting cold reason
Strip as gold as goddesses.

Give us such ease. O
My blue-eyed lover,
Why should your beauty
Alone hide in coverings?

Here by the riverside
The bindweed invite you,
And what more do you need
Than this light about you?

The Picnic

This is what picnicking is for.
Giorgione understood the scene:
A distant shedhand, flutes and wine,
Two graziers, and in the fore-
Ground such young women as Dior
Might dream of, if they had not been
So elegantly naked, seen
One from the side and one before.
Their loveliness is commonplace
To drovers summering in the south
And where's the man to take offence
At such delights of form and face
Even if you should give your mouth
To me in wanton innocence?

Here, under Pear-trees

Here, under pear-trees, on the broad verandahs,
Children like sleeping gods play games;
Surprised, awake in picture-frames,
Leaving a stuffed grouse, debts, and ten thousand acres,

An ancestral trick of speech or way of standing.
Their ponies with skinned-back lips devour
The blackboys, stolen in an hour
Time slept through, drugged by birds in the summer garden.

Horses and stolen roses, fine-woolled rams;
Frail youthful grandmothers who say
That things were different in their day,
Hearing the jets smash windows over the township.

Between the grey lake and the lyrebird peak,
A fleece of haze. Now tractors move.—
By careless roads of hate and love,
They go to serious parties, gay committees.

As an Old Cow

They're just spilt milk to her, these frozen shadows
The morning trees let fall on the cropped green;
And truth's not made that size. To chew over the scene
Is enough; then stump uphill in ladies' shoes,
Thinking yourself no more fortunate than other cows,
With a two-legged fool on a three-legged stool between
Your knees, a butting hustling calf to wean,
The girls in trouble and your man too free at the shows.
Little wonder she's sour, that she plants her foot in the pail
And stands stock-still for hours like a thing of clay
Among the frozen shadows. But when frosts are over,
Sometimes she will swing her head and flag her tail
And buck with udders flying through the astonished day
(For hills leap up!) shaken by life's quick fever.

To the Poetry of Kenneth Slessor

Dumb fumbler at the window-pane,
Your drowned voice sounds far undersea
Like traffic, bells — a fluid pain
Poured in walled ears, a poetry

That slits the tongues of stubborn words
Time and tired journalists deface,
And makes them sing like lyrebirds
And song give back the human voice:

Small words like worlds of musket-shot,
Words whose gilt mirrors frame our pleasures,
Words fine as hairs, numbed words that clot —
You calculate by weights and measures,

Then fish stray captains from their beds,
From smells of turnip-soup in galleys,
And front us with their formal beards,
Their rigid minds like bowling-alleys.

From tight-rope, tenement, and tram
You mock with fierce humility,
Yet take our frailties by the arm
And scour our linen in the sea —

The sea that like a mistress sleeps
Beyond the pane, and in your ears
Whispers with scornful timeless lips,
O blind man shouting through her tears!

To the Art of Edgar Degas

Beachcomber on the shores of tears
Limbing the gestures of defeat
In dancers, whores and opera-stars —
The lonely, lighted, various street

You sauntered through, oblique, perverse,
In your home territory a spy,
Accosted you and with a curse
You froze it with your Gorgon's eye.

With what tense patience you refine
The everyness of everyday
And with free colour and a line
Make mysteries of flaccid clay!

By what strange enterprise you live!
Edgy, insatiably alone,
You choose your tenderness to give
To showgirls whom you turn to stone —

But stone that moves, tired stone that leans
To ease involuntarily the toe
Of ballet-girls like watering-cans
(Those arguers at the bar) as though

In their brief pause you found relief
From posed dilemmas of the mind —
Your grudging aristocratic grief,
The wildcat cares of going blind.

Well, walk your evening streets and look
Each last eleven at the show:
The darkening pleasures you forsook
Look back like burning windows now.

Mannequin Parade

I

THE MODEL

Now Cinderella slips between
The mirror and the mercer's eye,
Slim momentary heroine
Of plots whose prologue is good-bye.

Good-bye! You turn for our delight
A face as far-away as flowers,
Brief blossoming of winter light
Beneath imaginary towers. . . .

And there the silvered princelings come
By stealth at night in motor-cars;
And you lie eloquent and dumb,
Watched by your silent cameras. . . .

I often wonder if those rooms
Were hung with stockings, would some young
Mechanic take you in his arms
And kiss you hard and wake your tongue?

II

HER GLOVES

Her gloves are pink
As the young coral
And under waves
She calls the sailors.

Where water moves
In the green peace
Of coral groves
I saw her face.

I stole a glove
From her right hand
And saw it die
On the dry land.

III

THE SISTERS

She comes again. That face!
Faces aren't fair; if I
Could look so, walk so, why
In that girl's place —
And please don't stretch my meaning —
I swear I'd be the mistress of a king!

I quite believe you. Kings!
Not one, for I would have
A dozen such in love,
Skylarking, banquetings;
And court and cabinet split,
These praising most my beauty, those my wit.

Choose looks, they're safer.— Well,
That makes a pair of us,
Married — worse — virtuous;
And happy to be so. Still
It's not a husband's charms
That keep a woman prisoned in his arms.

I sometimes long to show
Another man instead
How sweet I am in bed —
You know? *And I to know
Another's sweetness. . . . But
I hear the model's nothing but a slut.*

Beach Queen

Saturday. Dove calls to running wave,
Light rocks in the hammocks of the swell,
Dove-breasted. The city like a grave:
Flats without thoughts and clocks that doze —
Today, tomorrow, yesterday, forget;
In the dream of the humming-top forget
Landladies with slippers off who knit
Today, tomorrow, out of yesterday.
And the dove cries to the running wave.
The city's elsewhere.— Surely this is enough?
Blond multitudes upon the sand, a girl
Reading a book in sunglasses, the haze,
The acrobats and the ice-cream man,
The children building flats upon the sand.
The great ships drag horizons for her
And the tamed lions, the shouldering waves,
Slide to her sandalled feet and beach
The blond and casual to adore her.
Turn a page, how much more?
In her garden Venus walks alone,
Turns and picks a fruit, aware, unknowing.
For O the sense sickens, the sun hurts,
Sand rasps and sings. What do the waves cry?
Last week they swept the beach and left it bare.
What do they say? In smoke on the blue air,
An aircraft scribbles slogans in the sky.

The House Rises

They have taken their briefs,
Their griefs and their faces.
It's the end of a day.
In the garden a snail
Deliberately munches a leaf.

They have gone in the rain
With their talk in high places,
Their cares and despairs
And their confident phrases,
Their wish to explain;
And the delicate thief
In his back-street of slime
Waves an antenna wand,
Gropes with a horn.
Is it good to eat? Eat.
Is it good to eat you?

They have gone like the wind
With their grief and distinctions,
Gone like a leaf
Or the voice of the news,
Like death on the air
With a rustle of paper;
And in the garden
The blind beast chews.

FROM *Poems*

I

I

Hawk and Hill

When from the still crystal of thought
My eyes look out and make report
Of hill and hovering hawk, I find
They do but give me back my mind.

The hawk, the hill, the loping hare,
The blue tree and the blue air,
O all the coloured world I see
And walk upon, are made by me.

First I would praise the world of sense;
Then praise that sweet Intelligence,
The hovering far-sighted love
That sees me and in whom I live.

II

The Red Cock

The red cock crows within my brain,
The white sun rises in my east,
And blued with haze, the far hills shine
Like tawny lions in my breast.

The lion and the hogget lie
In my ringed shade and when the noon
Is blind with heat, my plovers cry
Like water from the stony moon.

About my heart the land is dumb
And quietly the habit grows
Of peace, but fires like lions come
And fill my blackened mind with crows.

III

Prayer for Rain

Sweet rain, bless our windy farm,
Stepping round in skirts of storm
While these marble acres lie
Open to an empty sky.

Sown deep, the oaten grain
Awaits, as words wait in the brain,
Your release that out of dew
It may make the world anew.

Sweet rain, bless our windy farm,
Stepping round in skirts of storm:
Amongst the broken clods the hare
Folds his ears like hands in prayer.

IV

Against the Sun

See how these autumn days begin
With spider-webs against the sun,
And frozen shadows, fiery cocks,
And starlings riding sheep-backs.

Against the sun, the rams reach up
To pluck the purple thistle-top,
And I've the year, it seems, to stare
And eyes that hang like hawks on air.

But tongued like snow, if snow could cry,
The cockatoos flake from the sky
With one black crow amongst their white
As a reminder of the night.

V

To a Ground-lark

When I go out to sow the wheat
A freckled bird with sticks for feet
Goes fluttering from sod to sod
And whittles songs of faded light.

The swifts are gathered in a cloud
And now in flights above the ploughed
Lands before there's green to show
Their pointed tongues cry soft and loud.

So let them gather, let them go
With sun and soaring, for I know
That when the wheat's about my waist
I'll stooping find a ground-lark's nest.

VI

This Wind

This wind as sharp as tooth of briar
Kindles anew the robin's fire
On rock and thistle, thorny tree.
Like a recurring memory,

And fixed in time as in a ring,
He shakes the snowflakes from his wing
And sets his beacons round the earth
As if his song had silenced death.

But O the flakes that fell last year
No rain will wash from Tempe's hair;
And where's the quail once tucked so warm
Beneath an idle Grecian's arm?

VII

On Frosty Days

On frosty days, when I was young,
I rode out early with the men
And mustered cattle till their long
Blue shadows covered half the plain;

And when we turned our horses round,
Only the homestead's point of light,
Men's voices, and the bridles' sound,
Were left in the enormous night.

And now again the sun has set
All yellow and a greening sky
Sucks up the colour from the wheat —
And here's my horse, my dog and I.

VIII

Winter Hills

The storms have greened the winter hills
Cropped close as parsimony, and ewes
Feed through the apple-gums towards
Their camp beneath the windy crows.

And there the lambs play round the shells
Of trees and leap in lemon light,
But the ewes never raise their heads —
There is one hour before the night:

One hour for dance and magpie song,
One hour to listen to the crows;
And here I danced when I was young,
And here I go around my ewes.

70

IX

Under Wattles

Now, here and there, against the cold,
The hillsides smoulder into gold
And the stockman riding by
Lifts to the trees a yellow eye.

It's here the couples from the farms
Play in one another's arms
At yes and no — you'd think the trees
Sprang from their felicities.

So may our children grow up strong,
Got while the thrush drew out his song,
And love like you and I when we
Lie beneath the wattle tree.

X

Pallid Cuckoo

Alone the pallid cuckoo now
Fills his clear bottles in the dew:
Four five six seven — climb with him!
And eight brings morning to the brim.

Then from green hills in single file
My ewes and lambs come down the scale:
Four three two one — the matrons pass
And fill their bellies up with grass.

But in the evening light the lambs
Forget their hillward-munching dams;
To cuckoo pipes their dances start
And fill and overflow the heart.

XI

Bindweed and Yellowtails

November, sweet with secret birds
And thin-voiced weeds that cheat the sun,
For half the season wastes its words,
But when my silent mood comes on

The little blushing flowers that part
The grasses where the sheep-tracks meet,
Go deeper than the morning thought
Of waking lovers or the great;

And those small singers made of light
That stream like stars between the trees,
Sum in an inch the long delight
Of suns and thoughtful centuries.

XII

The Red Hawk

The red hawk hangs upon the wind
And the wind strips the ridges bare:
All things go with it but the mind
That rides at peace in hurrying air,

And in the silence finds its voice,
Leaving like larks its songs behind:
The tempests come, they keep their poise;
The seasons change and they are there.

Blow then, and strip these blonding plains,
These delicate round hills. The blind
Are murderous, yet the hawk remains
And all of time in his still stare.

Song for a Wren

Today, to be alone with care
Who hates a crowd, I set my chair
Under some vines, when two cock wrens
Came foraging along the fence —

The first in grey, for his red bill
Still showed the yellow of the shell;
His friend I knew — this bird would sing
A song of satin in the spring;

But now how altered! What mishap
Had rubbed the lustre from his cap
And rich black jacket? "Come, Sir, tell
A friend why you are down at heel?"

"Friend," said the bird — a thing so frail
Might be caught up by any gale
And no one notice. . . ."Friend," said he,
"The season's not been kind to me."

"Not kind to you?" I cried. "My sheep
Produce no wool; the dams dry up;
My careful pastures, once so green,
Lie wincing under wind and sun.

"Not kind! And has the hollow south
Sucked hemispheres into its mouth
To whistle just for you, obsessed
By one pin-feather in your breast?

"The sun itself. . . ." Choosing my words,
I paused, my eye upon the bird's,
When something mocking in his tone
Told me my case was as his own.

But why this lightness? I had shared
My sorrow with a tiny bird
And eased my heart. With lidded eye,
He sang; and this is my reply.

Dear Maurice

Dear Maurice, Sure I understand,
You lost your bearings, like you told.
I'd not be reared here, on the land,
And doubt you. Nights are cruel cold
And fogs come sudden. Peaks are clear,
And the next turning, for my life
I'd not know man from fox or hare;—
And you were company for the wife.
While writing this, this minute, night,
Near twelve o'clock, against the pane
A moth came tapping in the light,
When snap! a nighthawk drops as plain
As day, and snuffs him.—This, of course,
Is by the way. Sincerely yours. . . .

Soldier Settlers

They hunt the standing green from sun-up for
Good stringybark for splitting. On the breeze
All day you'll hear, eating at hush, the wheeze
And tanged complaining of a crosscut or
The yelping of their axes. How they gnaw
At silence in the bellies of the trees!
And when high-up she shudders, from spread knees
They leap to watch green timber thump the floor
As if the sky keeled over. Then cleanly they
Lop head and branch and with iron wedges clout
The trunk to fence-posts. They can cut and lay
Ten mile of posts a fortnight. But the drought!
It eats into them — wire won't keep it out —
And has downed handier battlers in its day.

II

When Out of Love

When out of love, and reason goes
From bird to book and finds no rest —
For songs are silent, sonnets prose,
Unless a singer's in the breast —
I stand and stare at a green stone,
A hill, a hawk above the hill
That hangs upon the wind alone;
And suddenly my mind is still.
It hovers with the dreaming bird;
Below in briars the wrens begin
Their summer song, and at a word
All the coloured world comes in
With cocks and larks, and then I find
I have a sonnet in my mind.

Looking Down on Canberra

No doubt the world is carrying on
For Canberra groans in purple haze,
Yet it is good, these autumn days,
Sitting among the hills alone,
To watch a spider thread a stone
And listen while the mountain jays
Fill the distances with praise —
And every web and song their own.
The thousand voices of the town,
The worn phrase, the ruined word,
In this clear mountain silence drown,
Leaving the sweet song of a bird
And coupled stone. Yes, it is good
To think and sing in solitude.

The Funeral

Both priest and labourer, self-interred,
Here for a summer's day I have
Lowered myself into my grave
To wait the coming of the word —
And all the while a singing bird
Sang to her three green eggs above,
Having misread the time, or Love
Wishing that he might be preferred;
Till at her joyful enterprise
Grief faltered and forgot his phrase,
Lichen filled in the limestone's lies,
My dusty tongue took up her praise,
And the quick heart from fear and time
Released, sat brooding on a rhyme.

Fisherman's Song

There I would cast my fly
Where the swan banks and follows,
Though stars are foxed, the dry,
The vanished river's shallows —
And all of time in her cry.

By rock and silted bend
Where the buried river ran
And grass sings in the wind,
I would follow the swan
To the reach of her mind —

Till rock and mirage break
And stars double and float
Upon the quiet lake.
There I'd put out my boat
As the herons wake,

And tossing to the floor
An empty spindle,
I'd rest upon an oar
Watching the dawnlight kindle
Christ's fire on the lake shore.

A Song and a Dance

The lean man of the desert speaks:
Your hearts are stale from greed and care.
O come out in the desert air
And wash your hearts in the desert creeks
For love comes when the heart is bare.
We piped to you, but you did not dance;
We sang you dirges, you did not weep.

Another came with wine and bread
And sat down with a prostitute,
For she loved much though her sins were great.
Come eat and drink with us, he said,
For the tree is known by its fruit.
We piped to you, but you did not dance;
We sang you dirges, you did not weep.

For a dancing girl they lopped one's head,
And nailed the other to a tree,
And laughed till the tears ran down, For we
May tell this tree by its fruit, they said,
And give the lie to his mockery,
We piped to you, but you did not dance;
We sang you dirges, you did not weep.

Hear the Bird of Day

Hear, the bird of day
Stirs in his blue tree,
Fumbles for words to say
The things a bird may learn
From brooding half the night,
What's matter but a hardening of the light?

Out of this seed of song
Discoursing with the dark,
Now in a clear tongue
Rises his lonely voice,
And all the east is bright.
What's matter but a hardening of the light?

Mountain and brilliant bird,
The ram and the wren,
For each there is a word;
In every grain of sand
Stands a singer in white.
What's matter but a hardening of the light?

Sheila's Song

Over a land of stone
Goes the fanged stone of the moon.
What if I lie beneath
With this man and that man,
Tom, Dick, or Len,
Upon the granite earth?

What if I soil a dress?
I'll take the earth's bliss
Before I lie within it —
No more by night to see
The delicate honey tree
Spring from the granite.

For there is in desire
A cauterizing fire.
When I've lain with a lover,
I rise as pure and calm
As the slender snow-gum
Or the moon from the river.

Such Early Hills

Such early hills, the snow-gum tree
Sucks its spare blossom from the stone,
From stone the everlasting daisy
Looks back in silence at the moon,
While in the flowering tree a bird
Meditates upon some human
Theme as if burdened with the Word
And you, my dear, were the first woman!
Bird, tree and hill with scattered coins
Of flowers are in my embrace
When I hold you and through our loins
The river leaps, while in your face
Thrown back as if to take the sun
Shines the first wonder of the dawn.

Song for Odysseus

My love will have none of me,
She throws a ball about
Or scrubs her Sunday clothes,
Singing of some great lout
Asleep beneath a tree.

She wrings and pegs the clothes
And dances to the ball
At the edge of the white water,
Her call like a bird's call,
Singing of a king's daughter.

O my girls are scattered in graves
And the river has run to the sea
Bearing a tinsel ball,
But look, she cries, where he
Is battling with the waves!

Words for Wyatt's Lute

When she loves me
I love her least,
I'm sure to lose
When I love most,
My best love
She turns to scorn
Yet swears she loves me
When I yawn.

Look on another
Man and I
Will break my heart
From jealousy,
But let me kiss
Her sister, then
My darling is
My own again.

So praise with me
The moments when
We find in bed
This golden mean
Lest cheated by
A paradox
We die for love
Or of the pox.

The Beast

Enough! we cried and broke the beast
And shut him in a cage
And sulking in each other's breast
Smiled at our former rage

Until it seemed the beast had died:
We tore the cage apart
And ranged the staring countryside
Inquiring for a heart.

The beast we sought ran on before
And when we were alone,
He turned about with smiling jaw
And tore us bone from bone.

We Took the Storms to Bed

We took the storms to bed at night
When first we loved. A spark
Sprang outward from our loins to light
Like genesis the dark.

On other things our minds were bent,
We did not hear the Word,
But locked like Sarah in her tent
The listening belly heard.

And though we wept, she laughed aloud
And fattened on her mirth:
As strange as creatures from a cloud
Our children walk the earth.

On the Birth of a Son

for Andrew

The day the boy was born, the wall fell down
That flanks our garden. There's an espaliered pear,
And then the wall I laboured with such care,
Such sweat and foresight, locking stone with stone,
To build. Well, just a wall, but it's my own,
I built it. Sitting in a garden chair
With flowers against the wall, it's good to stare
Inwards. But now some freak of wind has blown
And tumbled it across the lawn — a sign
Perhaps. Indeed, when first I saw the boy,
I thought, he's humble now, but wait a few
Years and we'll see! — out following a line
Not of our choice at all. And then with joy
I looked beyond the stones and saw the view.

Hearts and Children

Let the magpie blow
Full round days like drops of dew
That ring the earth and dome the sky
And tremble lest they spill
Drenching in cloud-burst sunshine our high hill.

In the heart of dew we lie
Drowned in brief immortality
And watch our fair-haired children play,
As the bird in the nest
Feels her eggs warm and aching at her breast.

O lock these days around
When to a gentle oneness bound
Hearts and little children play;
And let such days atone
For those when we are many and alone.

Town Planning

The plover cries in air
For the town has grown
And hatched its brick cottages
Amongst the stone.

Where young lambs danced
By grave-faced sheep,
Five hundred pretty housewives
Wake and sleep.

Nine months later,
And not one day more,
There's a new baby-carriage
By each front door.

Five hundred children
And the nappies to dry —
The housewives gossip,
Grow old and die.

Overhead the plover,
Like the moon apart,
Tells his lonely knowledge
Of the human heart.

Mothers and Daughters

The cruel girls we loved
Are over forty,
Their subtle daughters
Have stolen their beauty;

And with a blue stare
Of cool surprise,
They mock their anxious mothers
With their mothers' eyes.

Droving

Down the red stock route, my tall son
Droves with his girl the white-faced steers
From the high country, as we would years
Ago beneath a daylight moon.
But now these two must bring them down
Between the snow-gums and the briars
Hung with their thousand golden tears,
To camp beside the creek at noon.
And finding them so sure and young,
The flower-fat mob their only care,
The days I thought beyond recall
Are ringed about with magpie song;
And it seems in spite of death and war
Time's not so desperate after all.

Talking to Strangers

Six Centuries of Poetry

To open up this lofty theme
Let's take a couple making love
In a tall pear-tree — Chaucer's scheme
For pinning young men's hearts above
Their pockets. See, she strains to him
And the spring day is quite enough
For mistress and for page although
A tethered husband chafes below.

Yeats walked on stilts for forty years
And lay down in a woman's mind
Yet wondered at the bitter pears
And why her mouth was full of wind,
Till catching skirts to block his ears
He found a girl with less defined
Ideas, and in the dawn his song
And she cried in their natural tongue.

The Stair

Beatrice, it's said,
Nowadays is worshipped only in her bed.
I'd not decry the spirit, yet
Lovers have appetites and need
More protein than in rainbows for their feed
Though at the foot, we're told,
There is, for those who seek it, gold.

Flesh is the stair,
Through bodies we
Transcend the body and are free;
So our first fathers struggled from the sea
And pushing back their kelp-green hair
Breathed the bright air;
So lovers sprinkled in a salty dew
Look on each other in a world made new.

Windy Nights

Naked in snowdrifts, we've made love,
In city parks, at the front gate,
And thought no deeper truth to prove
Than this, that lovers cannot wait.
What if the whole world disapprove,
Though it should be a crowded street?
See how instinctive lovers move
To get their clothes off when they meet.
O what do lovers love the best,
Upstairs naked or downstairs dressed?
Windy nights and hot desire
Or an old book and a steady fire?
Ask your mistress. Should she pause,
She has a lover out of doors.

Talking to Strangers

You can talk to strangers when you've need. I said,
She looks quite small but when she comes to bed
Walking away from her discarded clothes
As if she'd no more use for them than those
Goddesses you see stepping from a shell,
Or hatched like Helen, whole and beautiful,
She's big enough. There is a painted queen,
Twelfth century, buff and scarlet, I have seen
That's like her. Something dreaming in the face,
One hand upon a pageboy's cap of lace,
Her shoulders like a child's, each pointed breast
Tipped out a little (I would often rest
My head there for at times a man may need
A breast for a pillow as a child its feed.
Breasts are the universal comforters
Of young and old, and I found peace at hers.)
And then that sudden flaring of the hips
That's quite astonishing. My finger tips
Would travel down her ribs — when waists are small
They nip so close, two hands may round it all —
To find that lovely flowering, like a vase
Holding its precious gifts. Women are jars
Walking half-waking on the lighted earth
In whom the clamorous future waits for birth.—
Another thing, they all like to be thin
And naked they will tuck the belly in
As if the Lord when he first fashioned Eve
Instead of a round belly made a cave;
And this she knew. O you can always tell
True beauty by the belly's tender swell,
As Renoir proved. He did not paint the prude
But those who took the sunlight and were good.
We had our Eden too. Beside a creek
We'd walk together naked. Men may seek
The truth in many ways and innocence
Is man and woman bare and no offence —
A truth that they untaught us in the school
Where shame and shabby stories are the rule,
And the sweet body sweating in its clothes

Grows ingrained vices, fears, and crooked toes.
These we forgot and while our spring was there
Set gentle wildflowers in each other's hair;
When we made love, trembling with tenderness,
We blessed each other, having power to bless;
And as the fountain climbs its stair and spills,
Cried our free passion to the silent hills.

Words with Galatea

I

Since it was I, you say, made you,
The fault is mine if you're untrue:
The stone was faithful but with art
I broke to make your heart your heart
That knitting doubly wise and strong
You gave elsewhere to right the wrong.

O then a girl of fire and bone
Stepped out like summer from the stone
Who, subtle to take up my cue,
Swore she was faithless to be true.
So by those arts that made you free
And beautiful, you unmake me.

II

Your woman swears
At midnight she is yours, is yours,
Whose promises draw in
To the noon shadow that she walks upon
And barely shades her toes
When for another she steps from her clothes.

For those who guess
She strips the daylight with her dress
Imposing on all sight
A magic-lantern image, guilty-bright
As the lark-harbouring moon;
And it is midnight till the sun goes down.

Darkness and she
Return and straight your eyes may see
By her sweet body's light
That like a galaxy fills out the night;
And you're at pains to find
That they see clearest who are sometimes blind.

III

I am no man's woman,
No oaths, faiths, bind me.
Let slaves cry whore,
I keep an unlocked door;
Those who are human
May knock and find me.

Naked I was born,
In clothes they bound me,
Crossed my brow with water.
I slipped their halter
Naked as the dawn
Whose dews surround me.

IV

As I was flirting with a girl
Because my girl was playing hell
With half a dozen different men,
Swearing from me she learnt the part,
I chanced, as she came in, to turn
And catch her — I caught my breath —
There in the glass as pale as death
Before she smiled with lips of scorn
And picking up a painted shell
Studied the rare sea-creature's whorl,
Its involutions shot with pearl,
For fear I may have read her heart,
Then lightly set it down to pass
Beyond the scallop of the glass.

Je ne t'ai jamais oubliée

(After André Frénaud)

Without face or name, of water's colour,
Her eyes gone and the cheek's pallor.

Now that time's called the party off
And my desires no more accost
On stairs your shifty shiftless ghost,
I live on these poor pence of love,
Stripped and free of you at last,
A deadman with his private life
And joys he shares with rock and leaf
Now all our lovers' gains are lost.

Between the gentle breasts I slip
Of unloved women there to find
I lie down still upon your absence
And it's a living corpse I clip
Made so by you who are ordained
To blast me even in my silence.

Antony and Cleopatra

(After Hérédia)

Up there together they watched Egypt coiled
In sleep from the royal terrace. Muted alarms
Still flickered in the west; through delta palms
The river rolled towards Sais, black and oiled.

And, soldier captive of a sleepy child,
Through heavy mail, in his victorious arms,
The Roman felt against his heart the charms
Of her exotic body fainting yield.

Turning her face pale in its dark shore
Of hair towards him frantic with its scent,
She offered him her mouth. The East's dictator
Bending to her and drowning as he bent,
Saw in her wide eyes flecked with points of light
His life's broad sea and all its ships in flight.

Orpheus in Hell

I

To come so far and to forget the name,
When all his desert lore proved right, the chase
Leading to a vast transit-camp, a place
Vaguely familiar as sometimes in a dream
You think *Ah-ah!* — and there was much the same
Sense of conspiracy as if each face
Had just composed itself.— In any case,
Stepping from mirage, he knew why he came.

And then to falter! "Average height," he said,
"And pale complexion." They were very kind,
Which was surprising. Playing cards in bed
Or at rough benches, no one seemed to mind
His urgent scrutiny as chill with dread
He sought a face, a name. Whom must he find?

II

Dawn like a new beginning. Cold green light,
Cruel as water, charting nerve and vein,
Filled her like sap and she was young again.
Stepping from bonds of habit as you might
Step from old clothes, she followed with delight
The footprints of her guide across the plain
From which herbs sprang as flowers spring after rain,
And every rock and leaf were hers by right.

But when he turned and looked at her, the doubt
And longing in his sharp inquiry came
To her like chiller water. She sang out
To think that her deliverer shared the same
Needs as herself; and as she turned about,
The shadow that she walked upon was lame.

Mirage

The drought continued. By a waterhole
He played the shepherd: as the geese came in,
His kelpie staged the mob out and he'd skin
The green and dying, choosing on the whole
These tasks to silence. Not meeting with a soul
For so long, only dread and discipline
And water-birds stood friends or he'd begin
Yarning with his lean shadow. But control
Snapped when the horseman rode down from the skies
To amble through the gentle dust. In half
A second he was saddled; to his surprise
The other bolted; by a rocky shelf
He wheeled him, and in those inquiring eyes
He faced what he had come to find, himself.

I

Clover

(After Lope de Vega Carpio)

Clover! Jesus, how good it smells!
Clover! Christ, fill your nose full!

Clover and the young wife
Who loves her man. Clover
And the girl from a sheltered life
Out with her first lover.

Clover! Jesus, how good it smells!
Clover! Christ, fill your nose full!

II

Songs Through a Window
(Bavarian)

HE   Come, reason at the window
      I'm sick of cooling here;
      And if you've lost your nightgown,
      Then argue as you are.

SHE   Be off! My window's open.
      For all you've falsely said,
      Were you as warm a lover
      You'd lie like me in bed.

III

Waiting

(After Sappho)

Midnight. The moon
And Pleiads set.
Time passes, yet
I lie alone.

IV

Words for a Mirror

In this crystal oval wait
Sighs and snow and crows' feet:

Love is deceiving, none shall pass
Undistorted by the glass;

And when the snows of winter fall
The crow's foot will cross us all.

In the crystal oval wait
Sighs and snow and crows' feet.

V

Epitaph for Mrs Anne King

Beneath this sod
Lies Annie King:
To hell with God,
She had her fling.

Chansons Populaires

Qui belles amours a, souvent si les remue

I

Hey Jack, give the grog and the women a rest.
I'm ambling through Goulburn as cool as a trout
Though the chestnut is bucking and titting about
(Hey Jack, give the grog and the women a rest!)

When who should I see all dolled-up in her best
But Rose from the Royal and just stepping out
With this woolbuyer toff, so I give him a shout,
Hey Jack, give the grog and the women a rest!

Well, his look would freeze Bourke but I see she's impressed
So I reins to the kerb and I holds an arm out
And she's up! and we settles for oysters and stout.
Hey Jack, give the grog and the women a rest!

II

Change your love with your comb if you'd live a quiet life.
I shore here last spring if the truth must be said
But I'm minding my business and ringing the shed —
(Change your love with your comb if you'd live a quiet life.)

When in sweeps her nibs, the establishment's wife,
And she queens down the board and she's nodding her head;
Then she says, "Who's the shirker that's cutting me dead?"
Change your love with your comb if you'd live a quiet life.

"Well, a shirker, maybe, from being saddled for life
But you did not complain in the warmth of your bed
When you held me close as a bee in a bud."
Change your love with your comb if you'd live a quiet life.

Send No More Friends

Ne renvoyez plus, mon ami
A moi parler: venez y vous
Car messagiers sont dangerour.
(FIFTEENTH CENTURY CHANSON)

Send no more friends to me, my dear,
But come yourself, for friends may prove
A danger to the one you love.

Last night a friend of yours was here —
Send no more friends to me, my dear —
He did not mention you but strove
With every charm to win my love.

He has good looks and not a care —
Send no more friends to me, my dear.
Brocaded waistcoats are the wear
And his was of a shade of mauve.

If you send him again, I fear —
Send no more friends to me, my dear —
I shall leave you and him approve
He begs so sweetly for my love.

If you were sick, was danger near —
Send no more friends to me, my dear —
I'd come, as you should come and prove
Yourself the worth of my true love.

Swann's Song

While I doubted, I was mad,
Maggots coupled in my head
With the look of those I loved
On the gravesheet of her bed.

When in dreams she came at night,
Birthmarks stained her body's white
And a green obsessive fly
Climbed the heaven of her thigh.

Wind and water wore her face,
Rivers with a woman's grace
Wandered the green desert where
Willows wept her tender hair.

Led by my tormented mind,
I found what I went to find
And, a lucid lunatic,
With fair insults won her back.

Now we two walk out alone
Haunted by an undertone:
If this solitude is sane,
Lord, let me be mad again.

Thoughts after Superville

Famished giraffes,
Those lickers of stars,
Graze after gods
Through the sword-grass.
Whippets follow
Their visionary noses;
Tap tapping the dark
The blind root goes.
What are they to me,
Alive and lost
On sandbars
Of the Southern Cross?
Sometimes to a spark
Space gathers itself:
The cruising dark
And light of the soul.
Remember the earth
And what we'd say?
Green tree, green wave,
Children playing.
I would like to tuck
My memory in
And tell it some plausible
Eastern fable.

Reflections of an Artist

From my high room in hospital
That looked across the lake
I saw whole multitudes on wheels
Spin citywards and back.

Each morning mirrored in the lake
The slim gilled cars slid by
Of men who filled the office blocks
That on the water lay.

The amber city in the lake
Was shimmering when a wind
Sprang up and men and office blocks
Vanished out of mind.

In homes and lighted tenements
And bungalows of red
Shrill housewives stood about the doors
And swore their men were dead.

And dead they very well might be
Had I with brush and pen
And all the spaciousness of art
Not set them free again.

Love Song of a Lunarian

There is no need now to fly to the moon —
All the expenditure, this side of war,
Of money and men —
For I have already been there;

And apple-green in the lean air
Clowned amongst the eroding crevices,
Wondering in a commonplace despair
How long man can put up with this.

Then you of moon a new earth
Made and, midwife, out of pain
Brought me to rebirth,
And we're as wise as children once again.

Visitors

I leapt awake,
A thief or some mad-
man in my room.
There on the bed
Night like a possum
Sat eating food.

A yellow robin
Came to be fed.
The earth was silver
And the east red
Yet the sun shone in my room
And on my bed.

Next night it was
That you came in
Walking naked
Like the moon
That shines all night
With nothing on.

Dawn

(*After Rimbaud*)

Dawn in my arms.— The palaces were mute,
Shadows kept camp, water lay in its blood,
But watched by precious stones and in pursuit
Of silent wings, I followed through the wood.

For first sign on the road already filled
With light, a wildflower told me her address.
I laughed to see the fall's blond hair dishevelled,
Then quick through pines on silver heights the goddess.

In the path, waving; on the plains I told the cocks,
But, beggar, while I combed the marble quays
She fled among the belfries and the clocks
Till netted in a veil by laurel-trees.
Awhile I felt her massive body. Dawn
And the child fell at the wood's foot. It was noon.

The Boongary

In the night, they say, the boongary can be heard walking in the trees
Carl Sofus Lumholtz

On Monday night I went to bed,
A snow-gum sprang from my sleeping head
By the banks of the Grubberdedrack.

On Tuesday night it grew so tall
Birds nested there and made their call
By the banks of the Grubberdedrack.

On Wednesday night an axeman came,
He said, I'll ringbark your snow-gum
By the banks of the Grubberdedrack.

On Thursday night the axe did crack
And turned on him like a tiger snake
By the banks of the Grubberdedrack.

On Friday night the white sun shone
At midnight in my green snow-gum
By the banks of the Grubberdedrack.

On Saturday night in my branching hair
Grey thrushes filled with song the air
By the banks of the Grubberdedrack.

On Sunday night while I lay at ease
The boongary walked within the trees
By the banks of the Grubberdedrack.

Satirical

The Miracle of Mullion Hill

To Jock Maxwell

The cock has made his winter perch
The roof-tree of the iron church
And straining heavenward on his toes,
Turns scarlet, mops his wings and crows;
At which the Reverend Father Pat
Rolled out of bed, but reasoning that
The Lord who fashioned flesh and frost
And died that man might not be lost,
Would surely not expect his heirs
To catch their death while saying prayers,
He tumbled back to bed again
And prayed, "Dear God, first send us rain;
And then, should you see your way clear,
Rid me of the cross I bear!
Reive me, dear Lord, of Hanrahan,
The parish wood-and-water man,
Or else return him to the fold."
And reaching out into the cold
To cross the blankets on the bed,
He heard the cock cry overhead.
Then in his lean-to at the back
Hanrahan woke, and to a crack
Applied an eye, a shepherd's warning,
And seeing his reverence at morning
Prayer, he banged about the room
Carolling cheerily "Rolling Home"—
A ballad which, to say the least,
Is not fit matins for a priest.

"O Hanrahan! O Hanrahan!
Fear for your soul! I tell you, man,
This will not do! What, laying odds
And drinking late? Can these be God's
Recipes for heaven? Well,
Go to the . . . go and ring the bell
Calling the pious and the just
To Mass. And may the Holy Ghost

Descend upon you, armed with light,
And blast a pathway through your night
That shows more bleak and stubborn than
This winter morning, Hanrahan."

So saying, Pat returned to prayer;
And on the crisp and holy air
The bells filed out like sheep along
A mountain pad, ding dong, ding dong.
Ding-dong, ding-dong! In peals and volleys
They skipped like rams across the valleys,
To saunter home in single file
Leading the faithful up the aisle.

Now Hanrahan, you may have guessed,
Was one who liked his little jest
But did not care for Father Pat.
He'd taken up a contract that
He, Hanrahan, the undersigned,
Would clear such lands as were confined
By certain parallels and degrees,
Felling and stacking forest-trees
Upon that portion of the chart
Named Mullion Hill or any part
Thereof adjacent to the kirk;
With paragraphs on week-end work;—
A ruse devised by Paddy Ryven
To settle certain scores with Heaven.

So while the eucharistic bell
Tinkled like frost on Mullion Hill
And *Glory, glory, God on high!*
Rose to the green and luminous sky
On tongue of bird and tongue of man,
This sabbath-breaker, Hanrahan,
Shouldered his lean short-handled axe
Stained with the blood of chicken-necks,
And set to work. Quite soon the air
Was thick with chips; and if sweet prayer
And cries of "Timber!" do not mix,
What's that to him? Why less than nix —
For were not his occasions lawful?
But Hanrahan, you'd best be careful!

120

For, as he paused to flick the sweat
Out of his eyes and spread his feet,
He heard high up on Mullion Hill
The chiming of another bell,
A bell that trembled in the hush
Like winter water through the bush;
And then, as if the mountain spoke,
From orchid-tongues and granite rock
There burst a litany of praise
And alleluias! "Spare my days!"
Cried Hanrahan. "Another Mass!"
And stumbling through bracken, stone, and moss,
He followed the vanishing service up
Gully and cliff until the top
Of Mullion rose against the dawn —
And still the tinkling bell led on.

This was not strange, for he had heard
The mimicry of the lyrebird
Who kept a mound close by the fence
And stole the music for his dance
When tail a-tremble through the fern
He chased his bright-eyed lyre-hen.

It chanced that high on Mullion Hill
A ram was grazing. Two years' wool
Hung from his brisket like a beard;
He had a grave, a noble head;
And from a precipice he looked down
Majestically. The early sun
Leaping that moment from the east,
Gilded the shoulders of the beast
And set with jewels his horned crown
And so he gazed at Hanrahan —
Who falling down upon his face,
Cried, "Heavenly Father, send me grace!
Pardon my sins, Lord God of Hosts;
I never stole the Holy Ghost's
Communion wine; and as for trees,
I'll cut that out. Here, on my knees,
Behold your humble servant, God."
At which the vision seemed to nod.

So now when star-frosts glitter round
And bells ring out and hills resound
Calling to sinners to repent
And join with them in sacrament,
Who is it hands around the plate
And frowns should anyone be late
And swings the censer up and down?
Who but holy Hanrahan?

The Golden Cow

O'Malley was a columnist.
He rose at noon for breakfast, kissed
His wife, Melpomene, au revoir —
For a cab fretted at the door
And a launch idled by the jetty
Ready to rush him to the city
Where he would stroll from bar to bar
And roll his *Sportsman* and cigar
And snuff the white rose in his lapel —
And if a pin or prelate fell
O'Malley was the first to hear,
For he'd a feline sort of ear
And little birds who had to laugh
Soon fluttered in a paragraph.
While in return O'Malley told
Of his adventures in the field
Of love. O sweet fantastic women,
How fathomless, how feminine,
They are! Their girdles, gods, and gloves,
Their curves and cures, even their loves
Change with the chameleon of fashion.
Of late O'Malley was their passion
Who merely had to shake his head
To have them turning down the bed —
Or that is what O'Malley said.

So dining with his good friend Flamm,
A city vintner pink as ham
And full of the wisdom of his trade,
He chose a corner table laid
With flowers and silverware for two,
But one that gave upon a view
Of passing ladies where these friends
Savoured an ankle with their viands.

From wine to wine the meal progressed
And Flamm, unbuttoning his vest,
Spoke of exquisite private bins;
O'Malley jealous of his sins,
Swore there was not in all the room
A solitary sort with whom
He'd not the privilege of a lover;
He'd done, he said, the roomful over.
And so like gods they looked on Life.

"Women," said Flamm. "Now take the wife —
Women! How fragile and how charming
Their curls and lashes and disarming
Contours and declivities!
Enough to knock you to your knees;
But marry them and take them home —
As well loose tigers in your room!
Ah, there's a very different tale:
Your peace, your privacy's for sale;
And then to feed them and equip —
I'd rather fit a battleship.
All busts and balance with the men,
But sit out with your sister, then
What storms blow up and wreck the kitchen!
I would forgive plain honest bitching,
But starting out and snivelling home,
Tears for what's happened and to come,
Then martyred for the children's sake —
And when with words you've won them back,
Why then of course for a night or two,
It's into bed and tally-ho!
The meal is mine if you will tell me
How you manage with Melpomene?"

At this O'Malley brushed a smile
From his moustache and answered, "While
There's truth in wine, perhaps you should
Think of the hundred ways a good
Husband may prove his love. Take me:
I bring my wife her morning tea
So she may rest on Christmas Day.
I tell you, these little tributes pay
And give a girl an aim in life.
But should the fault lie with the wife. . . .
Perhaps we should meet and talk this over?"—
Draining his glass without a quiver.

So they prepared that very night
To plumb her at a private fête
For charity down by the harbour.
They found her smiling in an arbour
Where half the town in varying stages
Of truthfulness were being their ages.
And O she could teach the thrush to sing,
The way she laughed and cried, "Darling!
How sweet of you to come!" From head
To toe she was as brown as bread,
With little heavens in her eyes
Of innocence, and yet how wise!
How womanly and yet petite!
"Margo — O'Malley — Marguerite."

It was not long, of course, before
O'Malley steered her through the door
To lawns where caught in coral-trees
The city lights were all ablaze,
While high above in silhouette
A golden neon cow was set
Spilling its glitters on the tide;
So walking by the waterside,
They saw the twitching of its tail,
Fire bubble up and fill the pail;
And Margo sighed. O'Malley found
Her quite delightful, yet he frowned
And like a Royal Commissioner
Said, "Marguerite, what's this I hear

124

Of you and Flamm? He swears you're quite
Unbearable to live with. Might
I ask the reason for this odd
Delirium, for help me God,
I'm sure there must be recompenses?
Can he be fumbling his fences?
Speak, for his miseries are mine."
And Margo murmured, "Wine, wine, wine!"
Three little words, but softly spoken.
They left O'Malley's case wide open.

And yet so ably did he plead,
They found themselves inside a shed
Where fishing smacks lay stern to stern
And maidenhair and spider fern
And orchids dangled from the rafter;
And there after kisses, slaps, and laughter
And flinging pots and fits and frolics,
She stretched at last between the rowlocks
And with a sigh O'Malley had her,
Which may have rounded off the matter
But for a most unhappy chance;
For on returning to the dance,
Led by the smiles of friends and wowsers,
He found his tails tucked in his trousers —
An eccentricity that Flamm
Was quick to notice. Driving home,
He questioned Margo who at once
Took the most violent offence;
But when his suspicions were not pressed,
The silly girl as soon confessed —
There's no accounting for a woman —
Yet claiming she was only human,
She spoke of several times when she
Doubted his fidelity.

And when these faults were not denied,
Oh how she tore the sheets and cried
And ran half naked down the street
Returning presently to beat
Her little fists against his chest
And hug the children to her breast!

Till Flamm locked shivering in the garden,
Scratched on a pane and begged her pardon.
There followed mingled tears and kisses;
The dawn rose on their nuptial blisses;
And radiant at half past eight
In print and apron Marguerite
Tiptoed with aspirin on a tray
And drew the blinds and stole away.

And there once more the matter may
Have rested — it was Saturday —
But for a ladies' luncheon given
For Margo starting at eleven
Under the smile of Monsieur Max,
Where they discussed their pains and aches
Until the cocktails circulating
Set these merry matrons prating
Of one another and their friends'
Private lives and dividends;
And differences may have arisen
Had anybody cared to listen,
Which they did not; but girls must eat,
And in the silence, Marguerite
Was heard to murmur as she curled
A curl, "O'Malley's not the world!
Amusing, but when all is said
And done, I'd rather Flamm in bed.
I know!" And picking up her knife,
She praised the cooking and his wife.

Then curious arguments began
While others caught their skirts and ran
To telephones and soon O'Malley
Was knocking, a chastened Machiavelli,
Upon the door where Flamm lay sick,
Exhorting him like a fanatic
To rise and dress and fight at once
For virtue and for common sense,
Crying, "The thing's all over town!
You cannot take this lying down
For it's good-bye to love affairs

If women tell and no one cares;
So come out fighting!" Through the door,
The silence thickened to a snore
And elephants, it seemed, turned over.
O'Malley was finished as a lover;
And now when horoscopes are read,
Flamm is the man they see instead.

The Australian Dream

The doorbell buzzed. It was past three o'clock.
The steeple-of-Saint-Andrew's weathercock
Cried silently to darkness, and my head
Was bronze with claret as I rolled from bed
To ricochet from furniture. Light! Light
Blinded the stairs, the hatstand sprang upright,
I fumbled with the lock, and on the porch
Stood the Royal Family with a wavering torch.

"We hope," the Queen said, "we do not intrude.
The pubs were full, most of our subjects rude.
We came before our time. It seems the Queen's
Command brings only, 'Tell the dead marines!'
We've come to you." I must admit I'd half
Expected just this visit. With a laugh
That put them at their ease, I bowed my head.
"Your Majesty is most welcome here," I said.
"My home is yours. There is a little bed
Downstairs, a boiler-room, might suit the Duke."
He thanked me gravely for it and he took
Himself off with a wave. "Then the Queen Mother?
She'd best bed down with you. There is no other
But my wide bed. I'll curl up in a chair."
The Queen looked thoughtful. She brushed out her hair
And folded up *The Garter* on a pouf.
"Distress was the first commoner, and as proof

That queens bow to the times," she said, "we three
Shall share the double bed. Please follow me."

I waited for the ladies to undress —
A sense of fitness, even in distress,
Is always with me. They had tucked away
Their state robes in the lowboy; gold crowns lay
Upon the bedside tables; ropes of pearls
Lassoed the plastic lampshade; their soft curls
Were spread out on the pillows and they smiled.
"Hop in," said the Queen Mother. In I piled
Between them to lie like a stick of wood.
I couldn't find a thing to say. My blood
Beat, but like rollers at the ebb of tide.
"I hope your Majesties sleep well," I lied.
A hand touched mine and the Queen said, "I am
Most grateful to you, Jock. Please call me Ma'am."